FINGERPICKING
POP

ISBN 978-0-634-06539-2

Visit Hal Leonard Online at www.halleonard.com

This publication is not for sale in the EU.

HAL•LEONARD®

FINGERPICKING POP

INTRODUCTION TO FINGERSTYLE GUITAR

Fingerstyle (a.k.a. fingerpicking) is a guitar technique that means you literally pick the strings with your right-hand fingers and thumb. This contrasts with the conventional technique of strumming and playing single notes with a pick (a.k.a. flatpicking). For fingerpicking, you can use any type of guitar: acoustic steel-string, nylon-string classical, or electric.

THE RIGHT HAND

The most common right-hand position is shown here.

Use a high wrist; arch your palm as if you were holding a ping-pong ball. Keep the thumb outside and away from the fingers, and let the fingers do the work rather than lifting your whole hand.

The thumb generally plucks the bottom strings with downstrokes on the left side of the thumb and thumbnail. The other fingers pluck the higher strings using upstrokes with the fleshy tip of the fingers and fingernails. The thumb and fingers should pluck one string per stroke and not brush over several strings.

Another picking option you may choose to use is called hybrid picking (a.k.a. plectrum-style fingerpicking). Here, the pick is usually held between the thumb and first finger, and the three remaining fingers are assigned to pluck the higher strings.

THE LEFT HAND

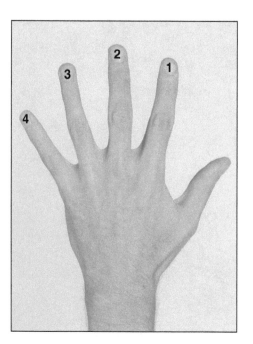

The left-hand fingers are numbered 1 through 4.

Be sure to keep your fingers arched, with each joint bent; if they flatten out across the strings, they will deaden the sound when you fingerpick. As a general rule, let the strings ring as long as possible when playing fingerstyle.

Can You Feel the Love Tonight

from Walt Disney Pictures' THE LION KING

Music by Elton John
Lyrics by Tim Rice

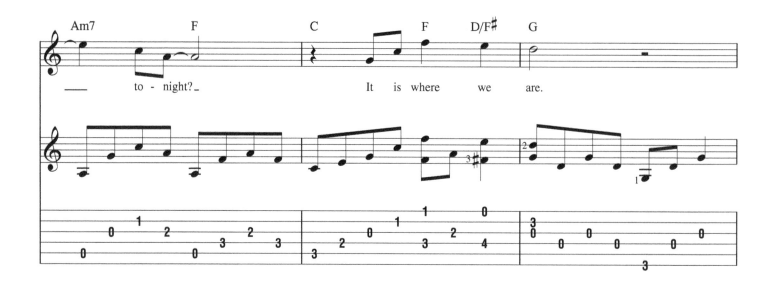

to - night? It is where we are.

It's e - nough for this wide - eyed wan - der - er that we got this

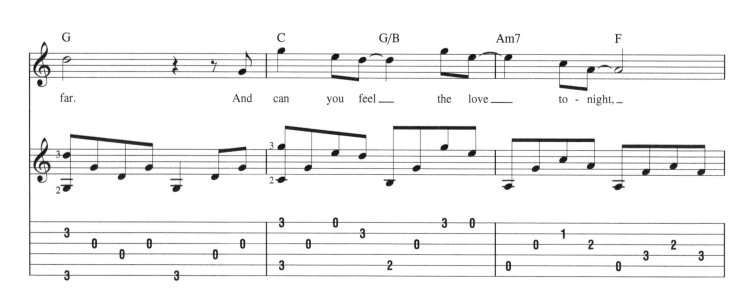

far. And can you feel the love to - night,

how it's laid to rest? It's e-nough to make

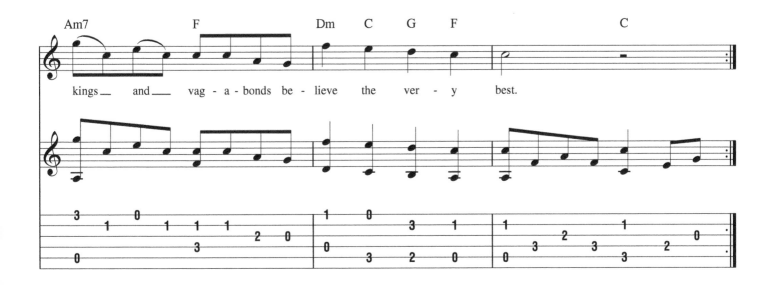

kings_ and_ vag-a-bonds be-lieve the ver-y best.

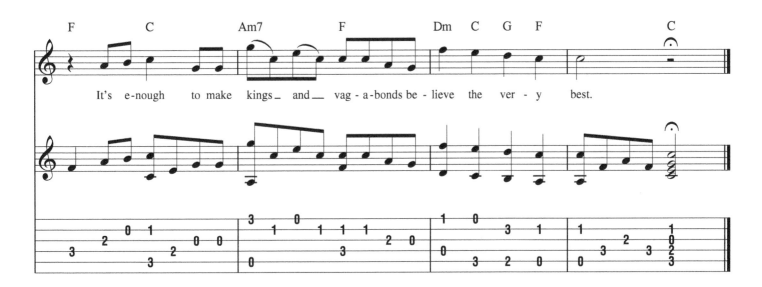

It's e-nough to make kings_ and_ vag-a-bonds be-lieve the ver-y best.

Don't Know Why

Words and Music by Jesse Harris

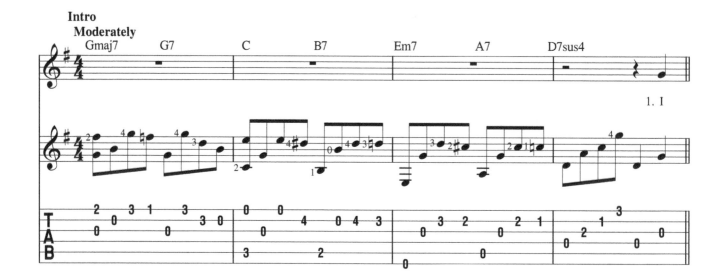

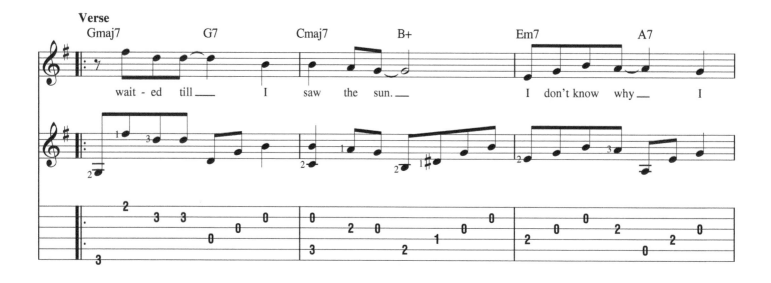

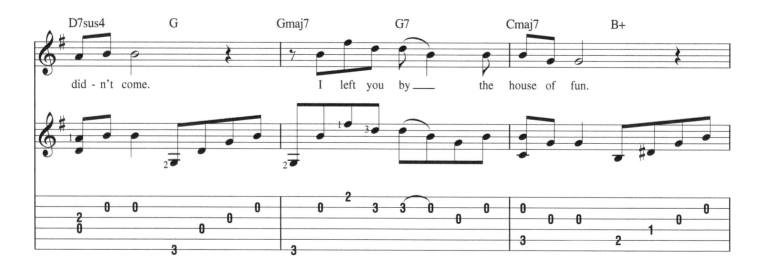

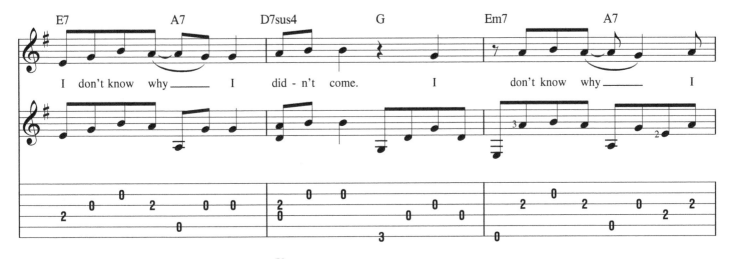

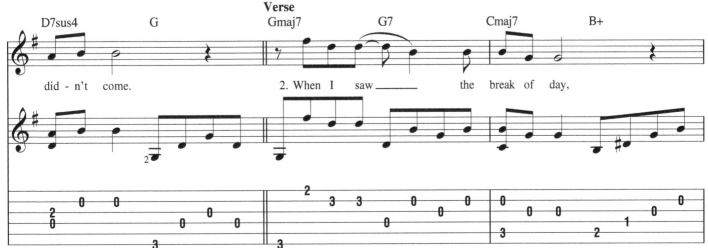

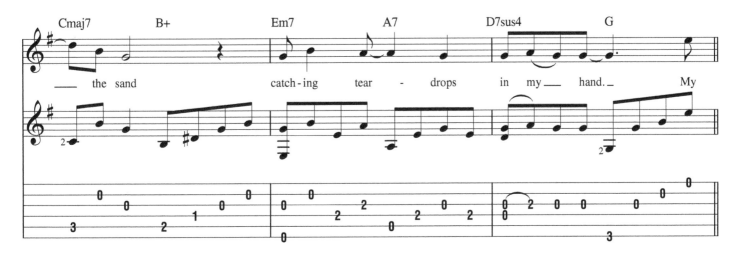

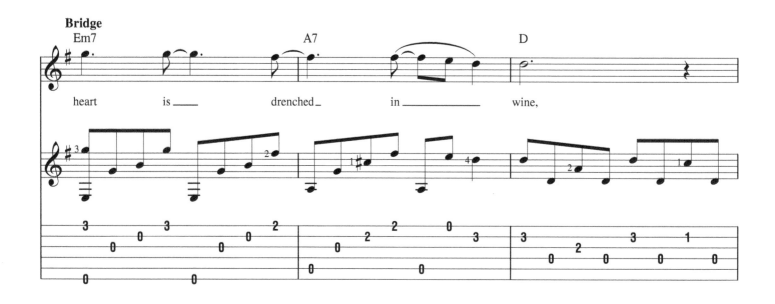

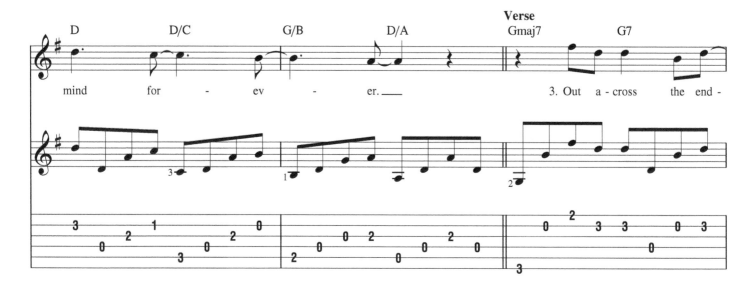

- less sea, I would die _____ in ec - sta - sy.

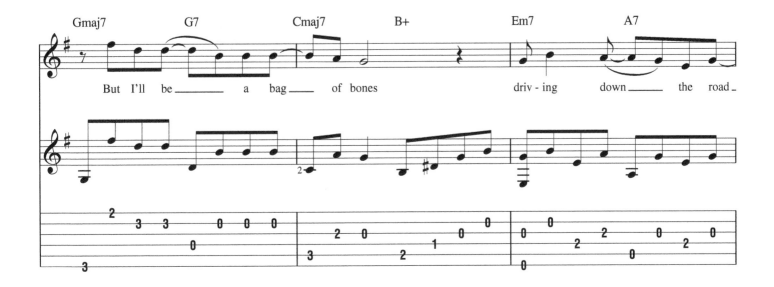

But I'll be _____ a bag _____ of bones driv - ing down _____ the road _____

Bridge

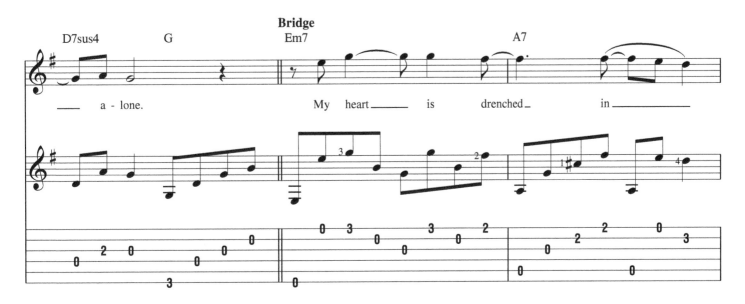

_____ a - lone. My heart _____ is drenched _ in _____

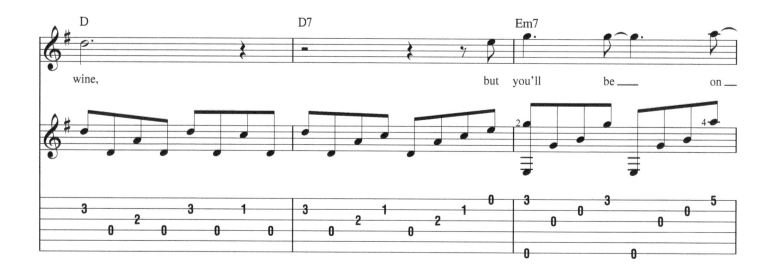

wine,   but you'll   be ___   on ___

___ my ___ mind   for   -   ev   -   er. ___

Interlude

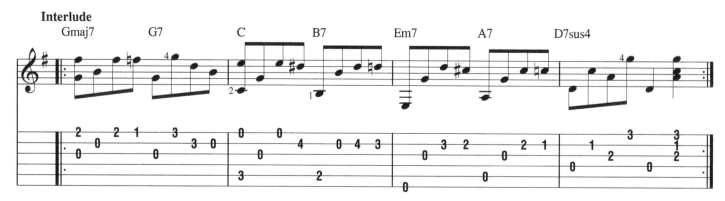

Outro-Verse

Some-thing has ___ to   make ___ you   run. ___   I   don't know why ___ I

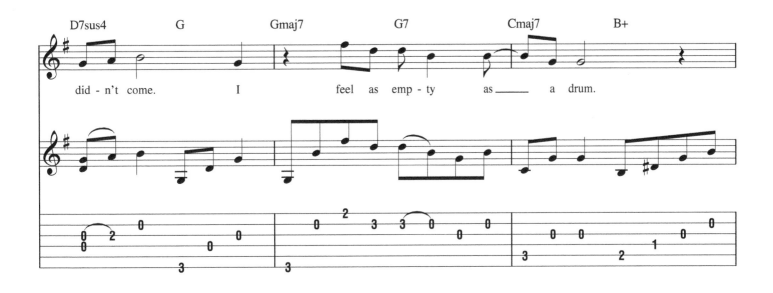

Endless Love

Words and Music by Lionel Richie

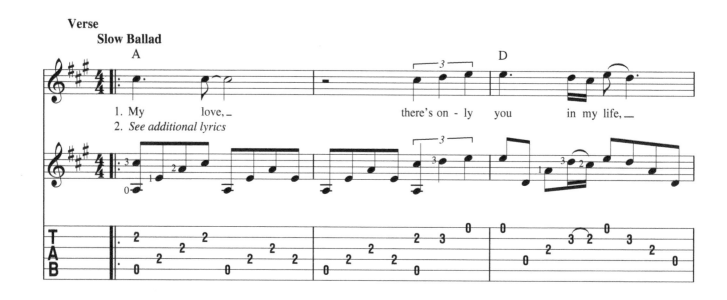

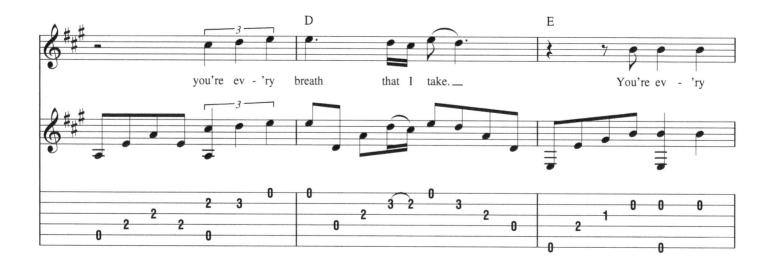

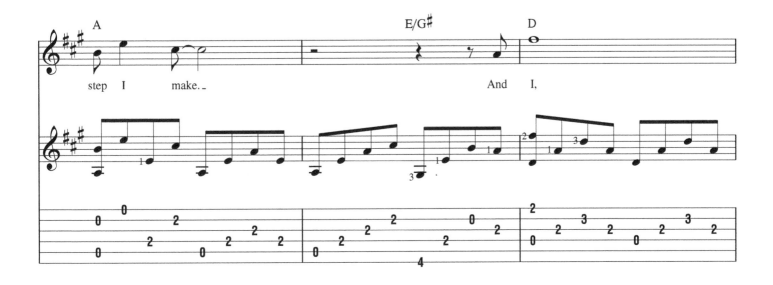

step I make.   And I,

I want to share all my love ———————— with you.

No one else will _ do.   And your eyes, _

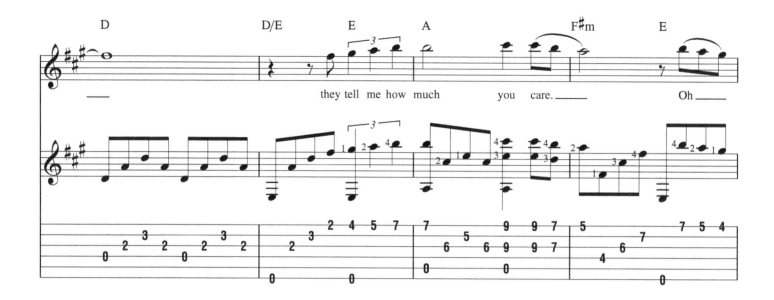

they tell me how much you care.___ Oh___

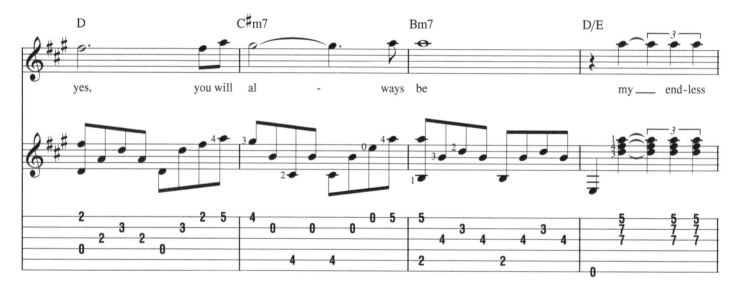

yes, you will al - ways be my ___ end-less

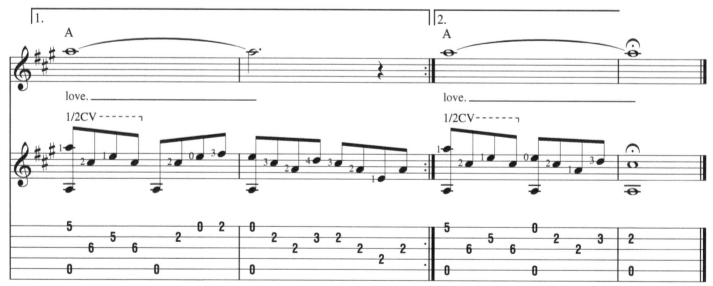

1. love.___

2. love.___

Additional Lyrics

2. Two hearts, two hearts that beat as one.
   Our lives have just begun.
   Forever I'll hold you close in my arms.
   I can't resist your charm.
   And love, I'll be a fool for you, I'm sure.
   You know I don't mind.
   'Cause you, you mean the world to me.
   Oh yes, I've found in you my endless love.

I'll Be

Words and Music by Edwin McCain

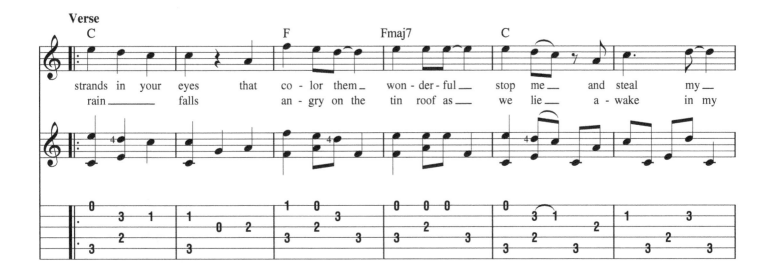

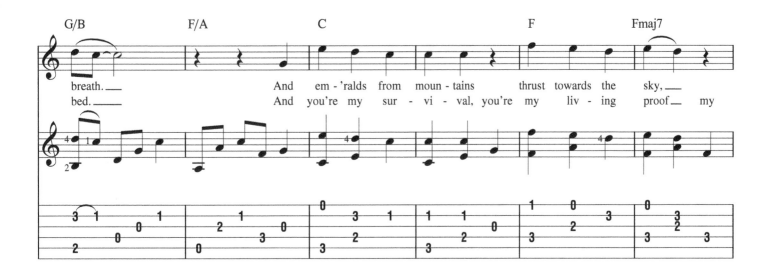

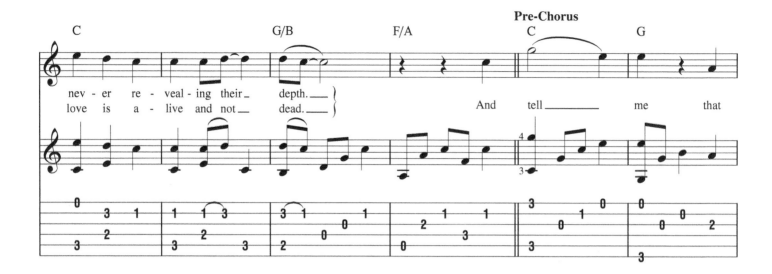

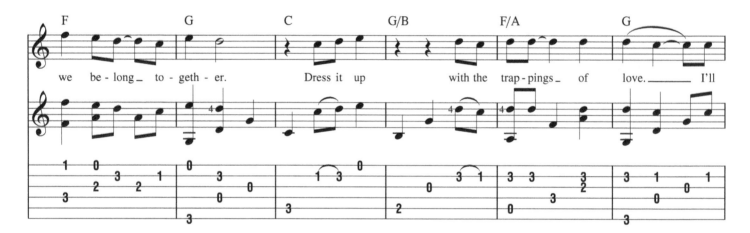

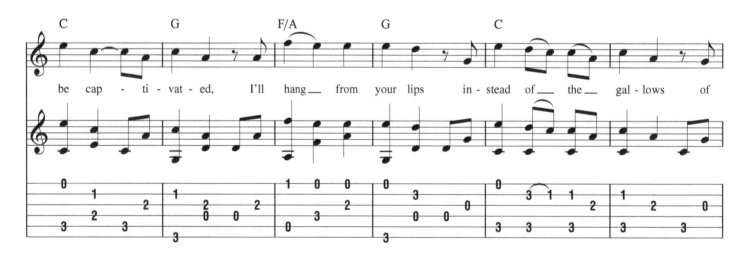

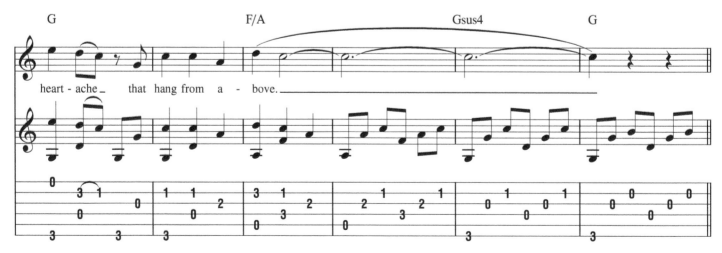

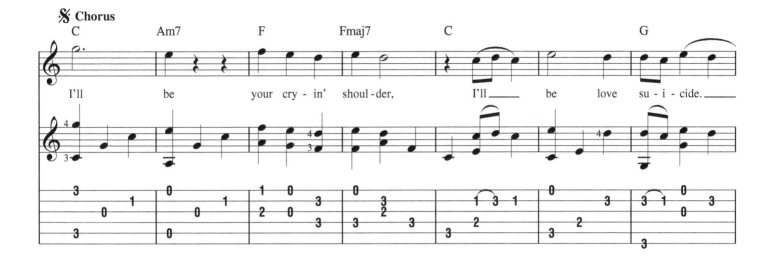

I'll be your cry-in' shoul-der, I'll ___ be love su-i-cide. ___

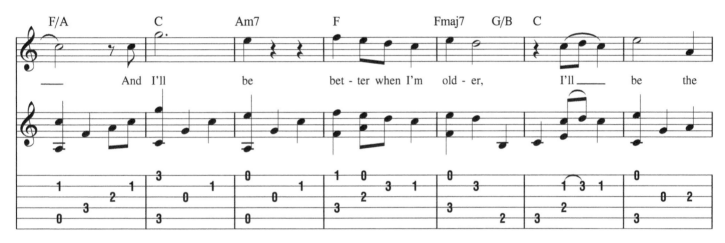

And I'll be bet-ter when I'm old-er, I'll ___ be the

To Coda ⊕

1.

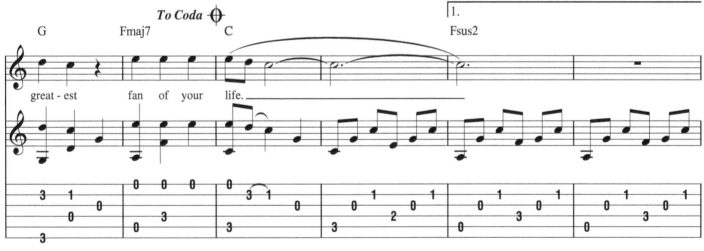

great-est fan of your life. ___

2.

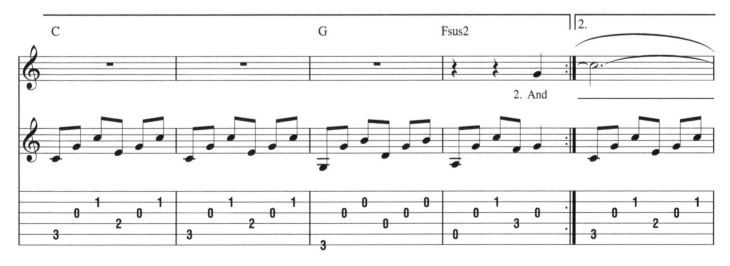

2. And ___

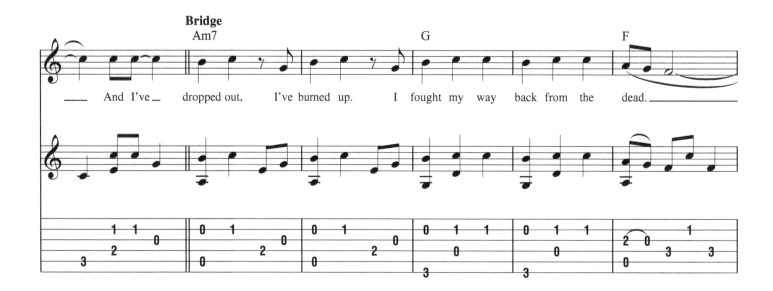

Bridge

And I've dropped out, I've burned up. I fought my way back from the dead.

I've tuned in, turned on, re-

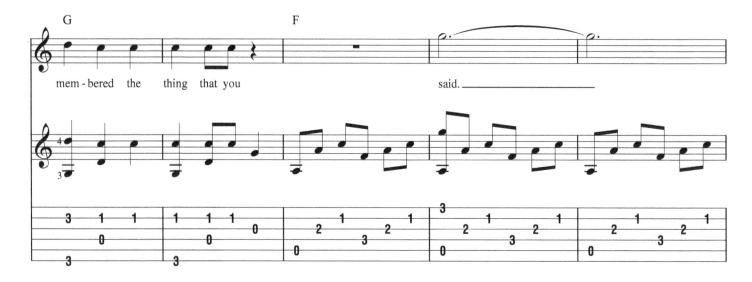

mem-bered the thing that you said.

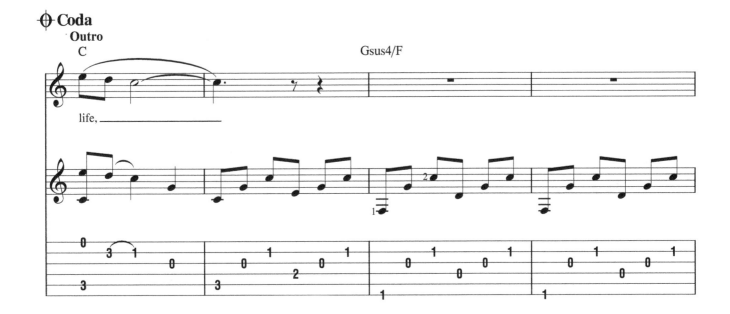

Every Breath You Take

Music and Lyrics by Sting

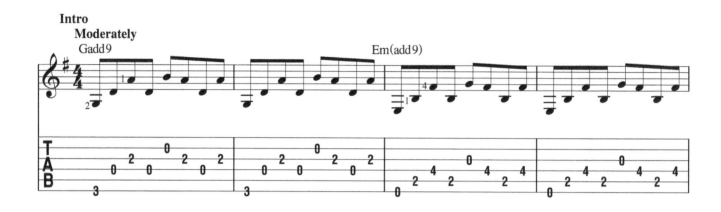

1. Ev -'ry breath you

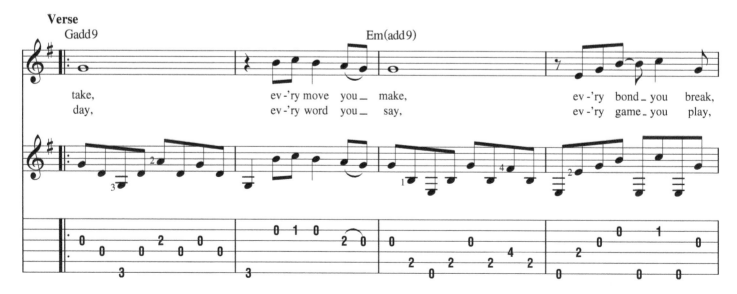

take,
day,

ev -'ry move you __ make,
ev -'ry word you __ say,

ev -'ry bond __ you break,
ev -'ry game __ you play,

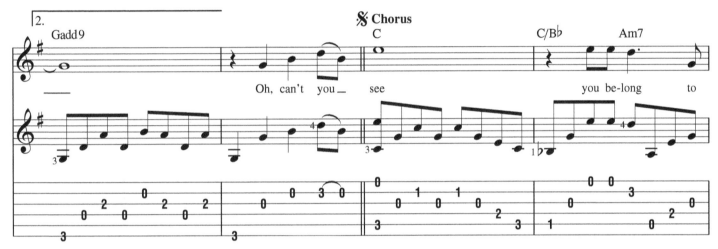

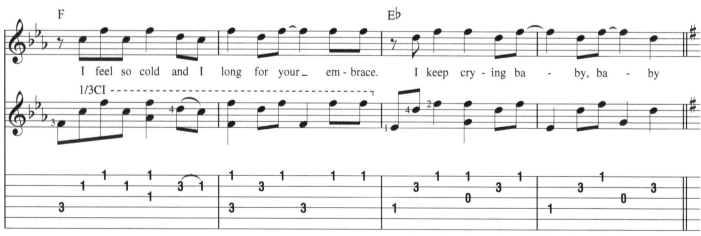

Interlude

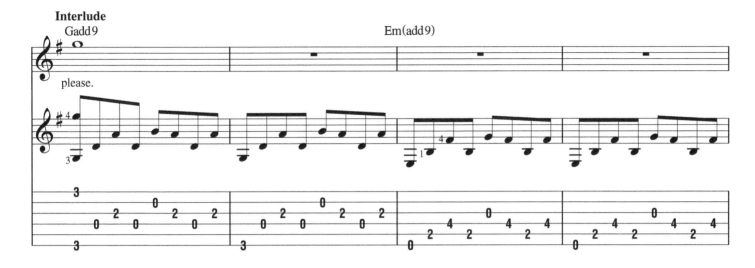

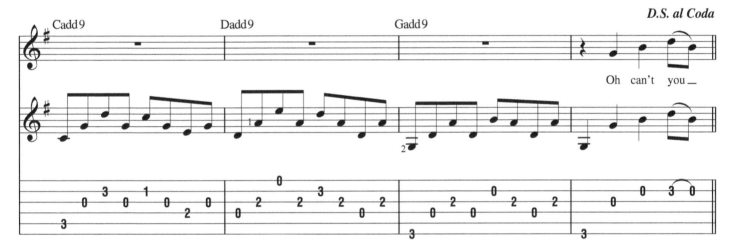

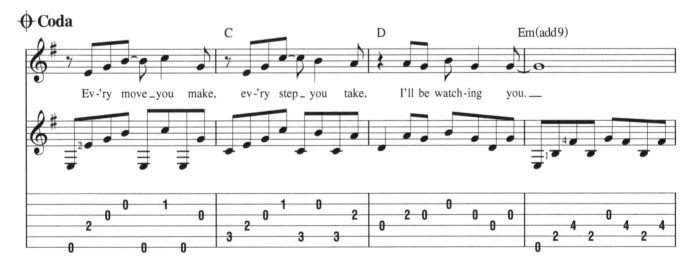

Imagine

Words and Music by John Lennon

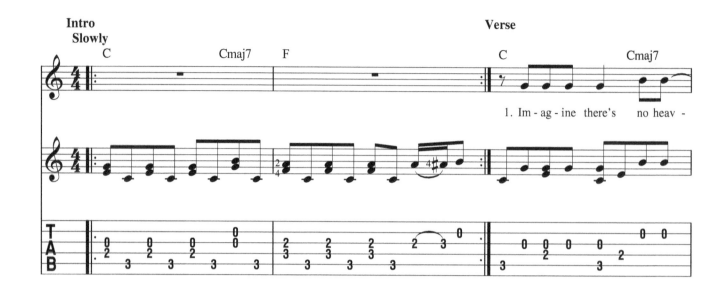

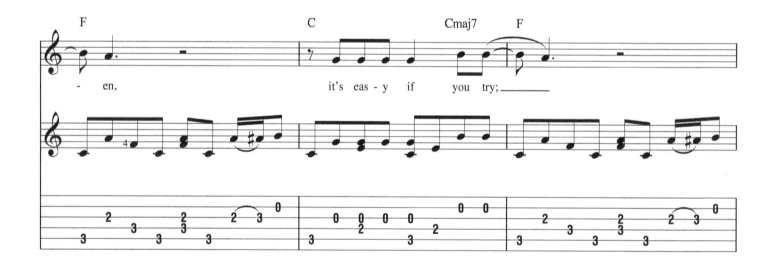

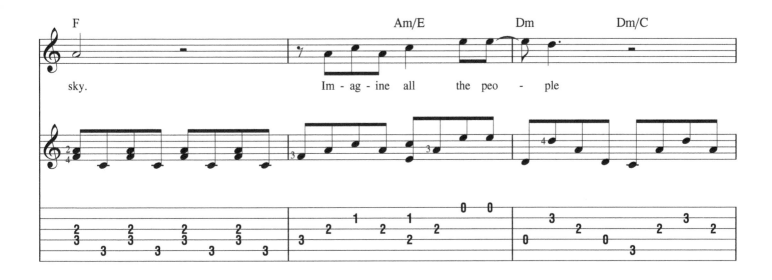

sky.

Im - ag - ine all the peo - ple

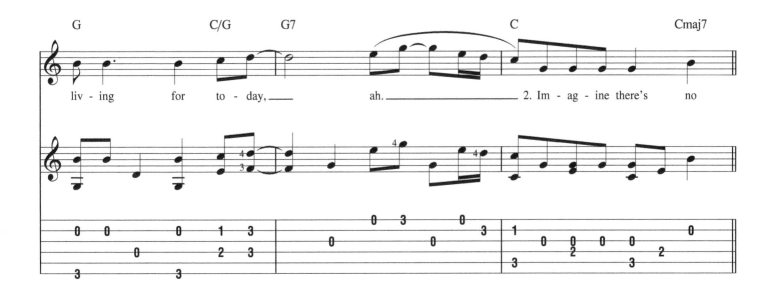

liv - ing for to - day, ____ ah. ____ 2. Im - ag - ine there's no

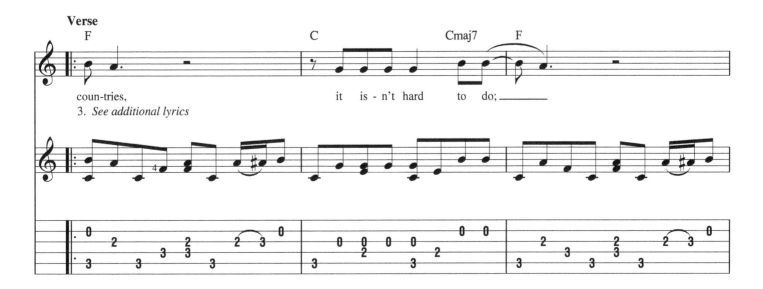

Verse

coun-tries,
3. *See additional lyrics*

it is - n't hard to do; ____

dream - er, but I'm not the on - ly one.

I hope some day you'll_ join us and the world_____ will

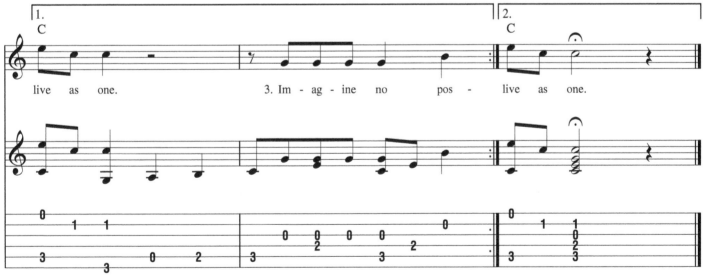

1.

live as one. 3. Im - ag - ine no pos - live as one.

Additional Lyrics

3. Imagine no possessions,
   I wonder if you can;
   No need for greed or hunger,
   A brotherhood of man.
   Imagine all the people sharing all the world.

Leader of the Band

Words and Music by Dan Fogelberg

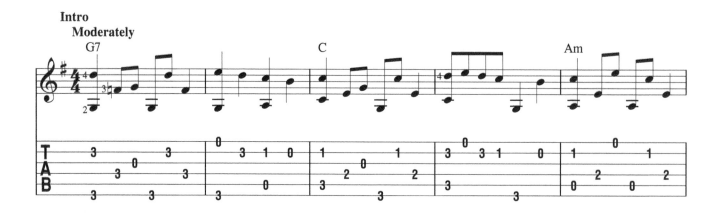

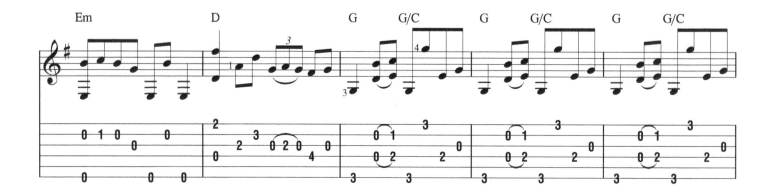

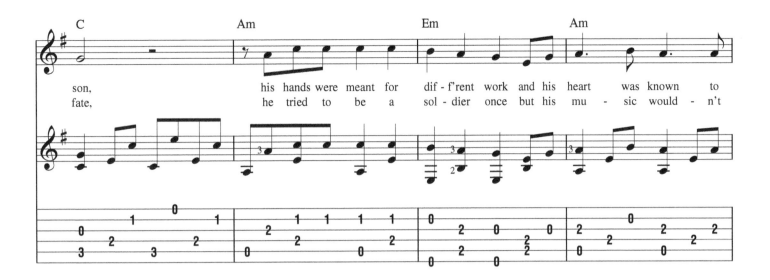

son,   his hands were meant for dif-f'rent work and his heart was known to
fate,   he tried to be a sol-dier once but his mu-sic would-n't

none. _____   He left his home and went his lone __ and sol-i-tar-y
wait. _____   He earned his love through dis-ci-pline,__ a thun-d'ring vel-vet

To Coda 1 ⊕

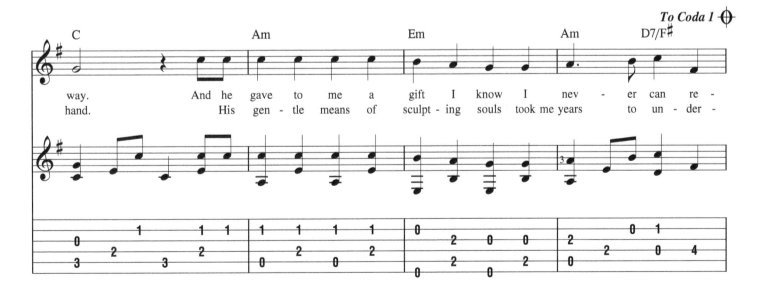

way.   And he gave to me a gift I know I nev-er can re-
hand.   His gen-tle means of sculpt-ing souls took me years to un-der-

Chorus

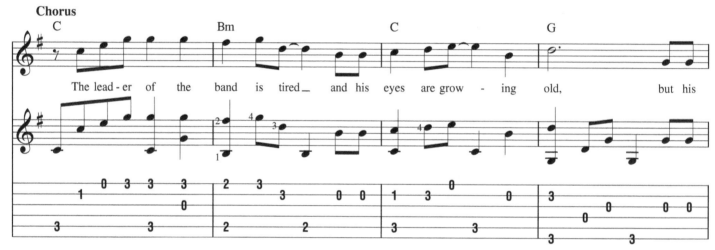

The lead-er of the band is tired_ and his eyes are grow - ing old, but his

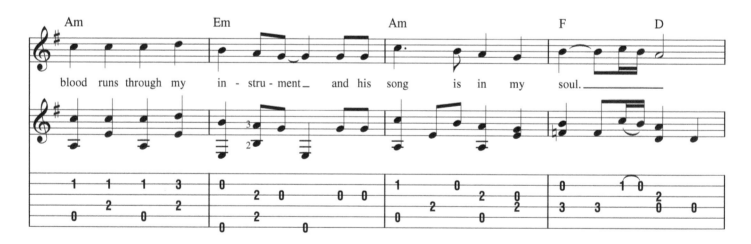

blood runs through my in - stru - ment_ and his song is in my soul. _____

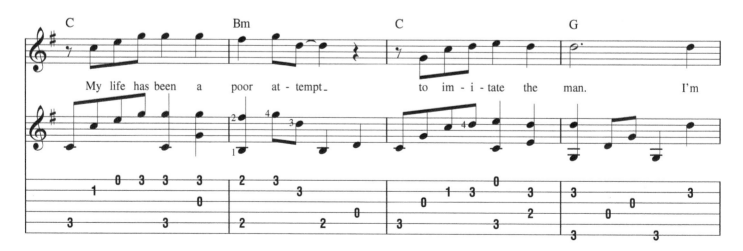

My life has been a poor at - tempt_ to im - i - tate the man. I'm

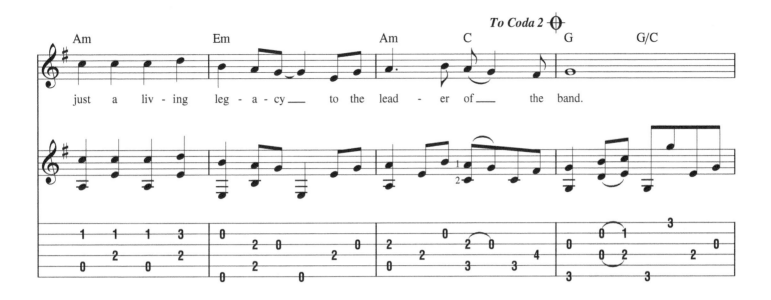

just a liv-ing leg-a-cy ___ to the lead - er of ___ the band.

D.S. al Coda 1

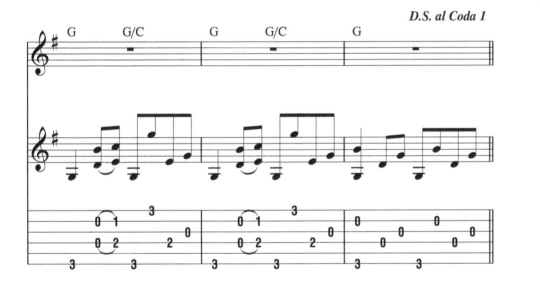

⊕ Coda 1

well.

⊕ Coda 2

D.C. al Coda 2
(take 2nd ending)

band. I am the liv-ing leg-a-cy ___ to the

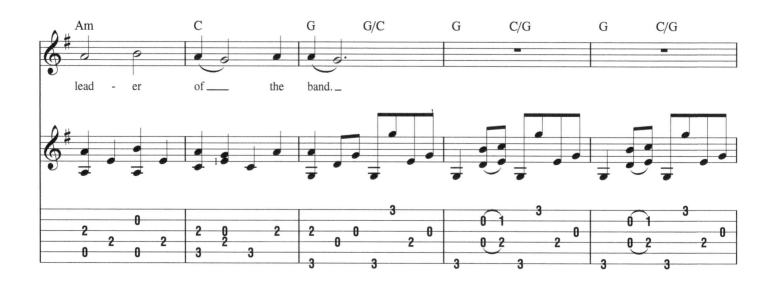

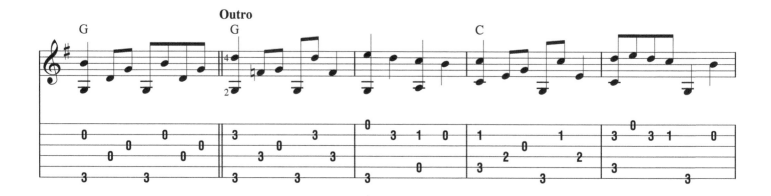

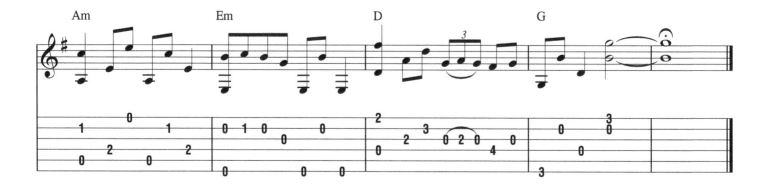

Additional Lyrics

3. My brothers' lives were diff'rent for they heard another call.
One went to Chicago, and the other to St. Paul.
And I'm in Colorado when I'm not in some hotel,
Living out this life I chose and come to know so well.

4. I thank you for the music and your stories of the road.
I thank you for the freedom when it came my time to go.
I thank you for the kindness and the times when you got tough.
And Papa, I don't think I said "I love you" near enough.

My Cherie Amour

Words and Music by Stevie Wonder, Sylvia Moy and Henry Cosby

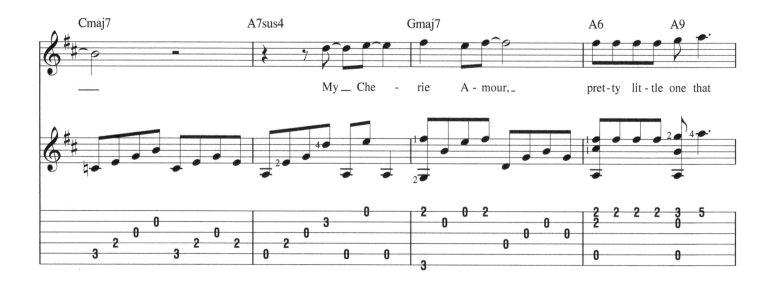

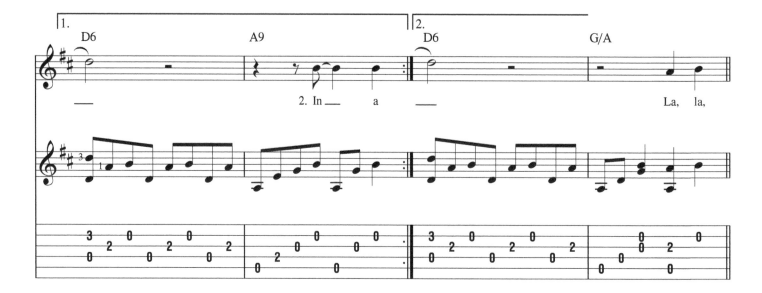

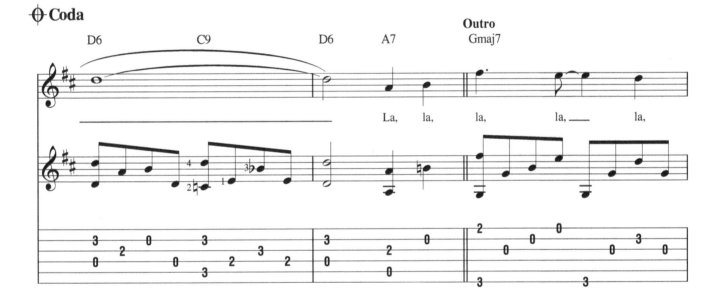

Additional Lyrics

2. In a café or sometimes on a crowded street,
   I've been near you but you never noticed me.
   My Cherie Amour, won't you tell me how could you ignore,
   That behind that little smile I wore,
   How I wish that you were mine.

3. Maybe someday, you'll see my face among the crowd.
   Maybe someday, I'll share your little distant cloud.
   Oh, Cherie Amour, pretty little one that I adore,
   You're the only girl my heart beats for;
   How I wish that you were mine.

Let It Be

Words and Music by John Lennon and Paul McCartney

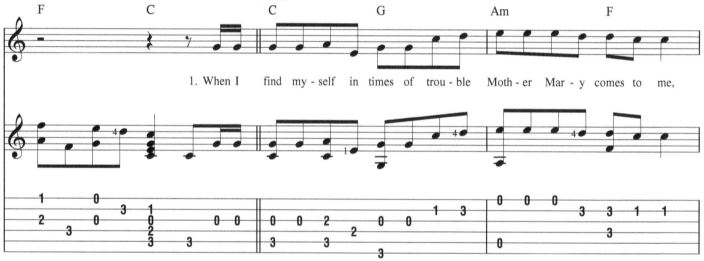

standing right in front of me, speaking words of wisdom, let it be. Let it

Chorus

be, let it be, let it be, let it be. Whisper words of wisdom, let it

Verse

be. 2. And when the broken-hearted people living in the world agree,
3. *See additional lyrics*

there will be an an - swer, let it be. ___ For though they may be part - ed, there is

still a chance that they will see. There will be an an - swer, let it be. ___ Let it

Chorus

be, let it be, ___ let it be, ___ let it be. There will be an an - swer, let it

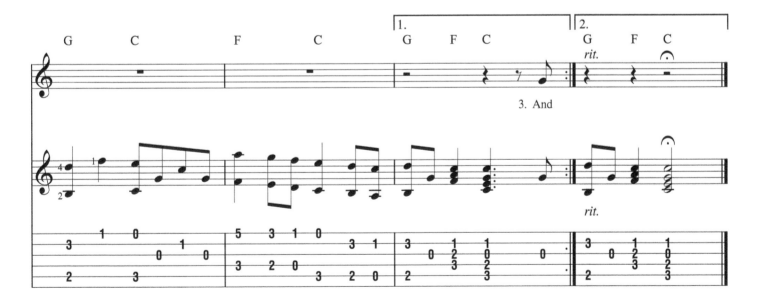

Additional Lyrics

3. And when the night is cloudy, there is still a light that shines on me,
   Shine until tomorrow, let it be.
   I wake up to the sound of music, Mother Mary comes to me,
   Speaking words of wisdom, let it be.

My Heart Will Go On

(Love Theme from 'Titanic')

from the Paramount and Twentieth Century Fox Motion Picture TITANIC

Music by James Horner
Lyric by Will Jennings

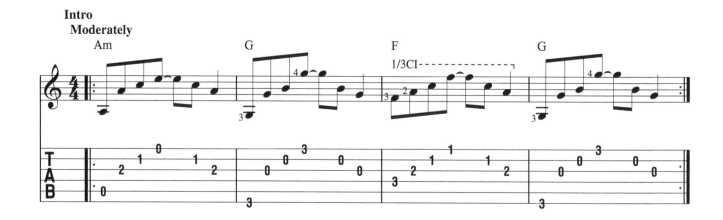

1. Ev - 'ry night in my dreams I see you, I feel you,
2. Love can touch us one time and last for a life - time,

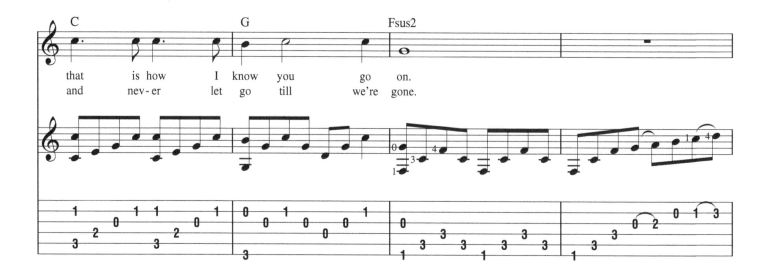

that is how I know you go on.
and nev - er let go till we're gone.

Far a-cross the dis - tance and spac - es be - tween us
Love was when I loved you; one true time I hold to.

you have come to show you go on.
In my life we'll al - ways go on.

Chorus

Near, far, wher - ev - er you are, I be -

lieve   that   the   heart does   go   on.

Once   more   you   o - pen the door   and you're

here   in my heart, and   my heart will   go   on   and

Outro-Chorus

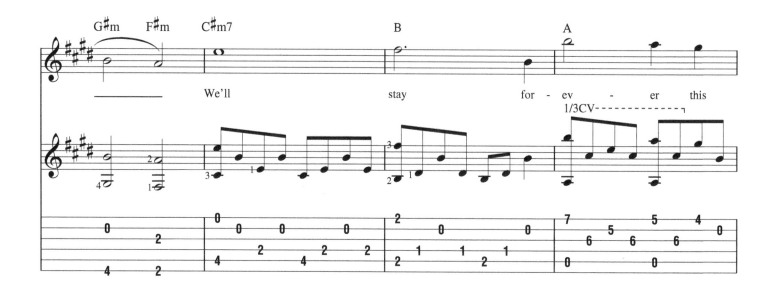

We'll stay forever this

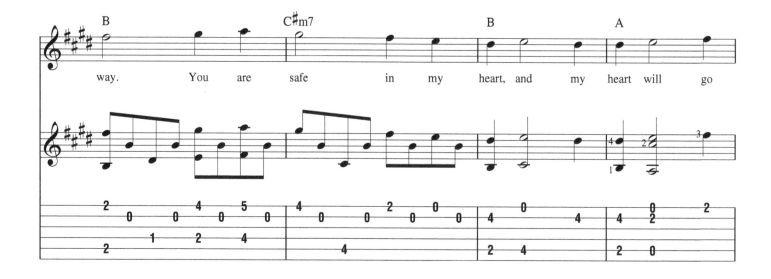

way. You are safe in my heart, and my heart will go

on and on.

Stand by Me

Words and Music by Ben E. King, Jerry Leiber and Mike Stoller

won't   be a - fraid,   no, I ___ won't   be a - fraid   just as

long _____ as you stand, _____ stand by me.   So, dar - ling, dar - ling

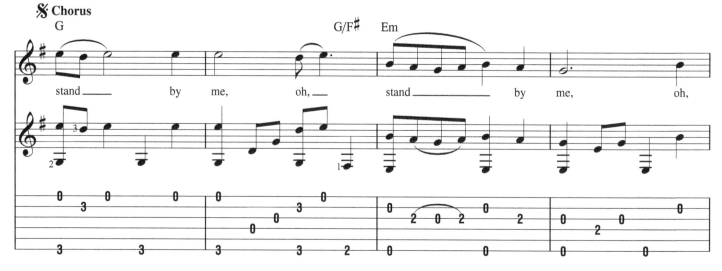

𝄋 **Chorus**

stand _____ by me,   oh, ___   stand _____ by me,   oh,

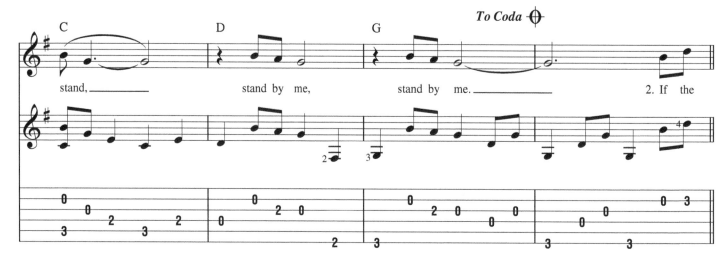

To Coda ⊕

stand, _____   stand by me,   stand by me. _____   2. If the

48

Piano Man

Words and Music by Billy Joel

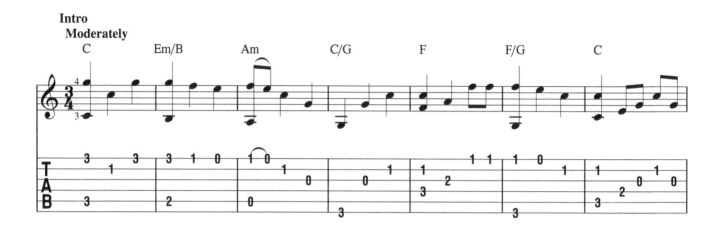

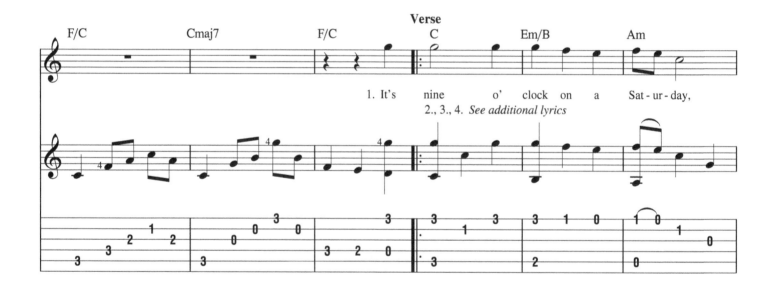

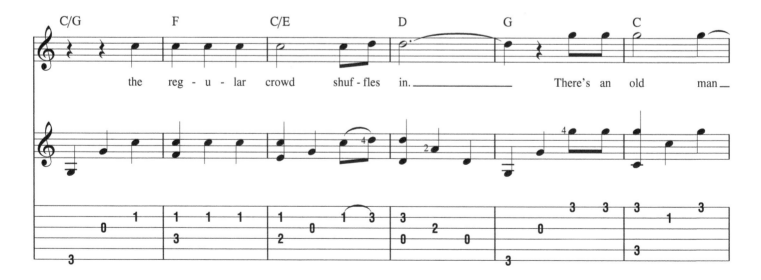

sit-ting next to me _____ mak-in' love to his ton-ic and gin.

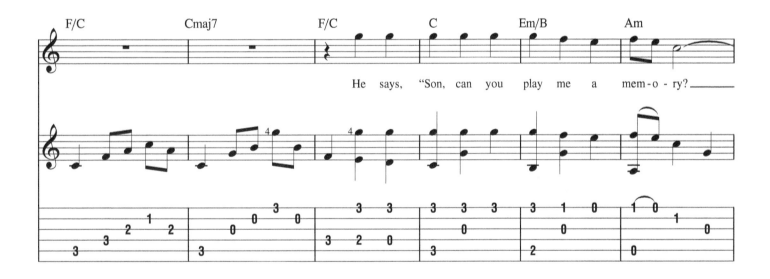

He says, "Son, can you play me a mem-o-ry? _____

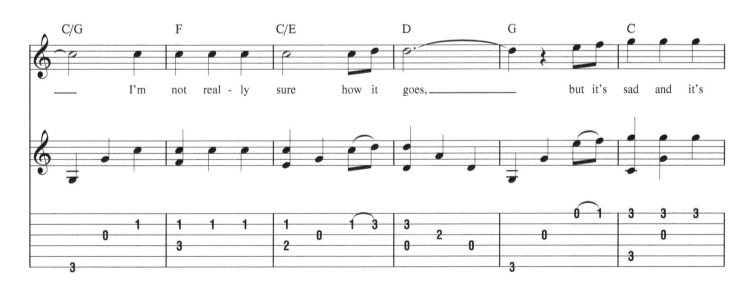

_____ I'm not real-ly sure how it goes, _____ but it's sad and it's

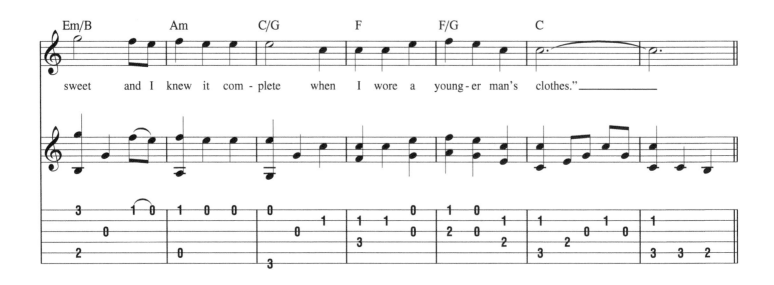

sweet and I knew it com-plete when I wore a young-er man's clothes."

Bridge

Da, da, da, de, de, da. ___ Da, da, de, de,

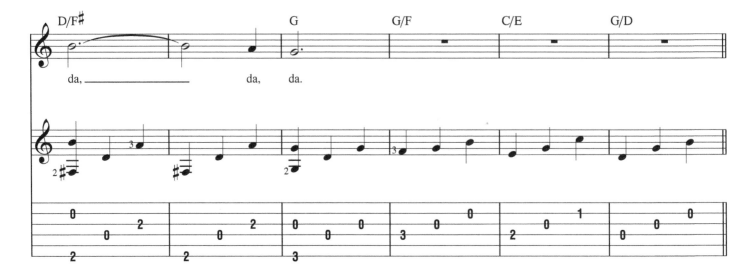

da, ___ da, da.

Chorus

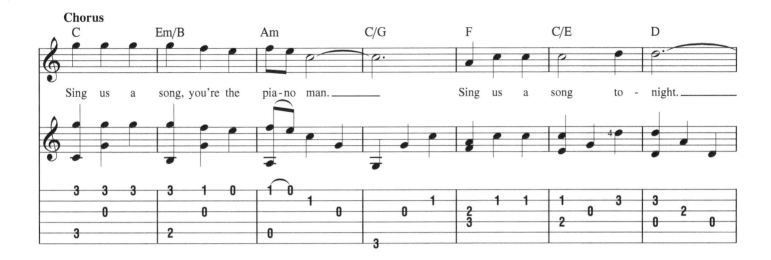

Sing us a song, you're the pia-no man. _____ Sing us a song to - night. _____

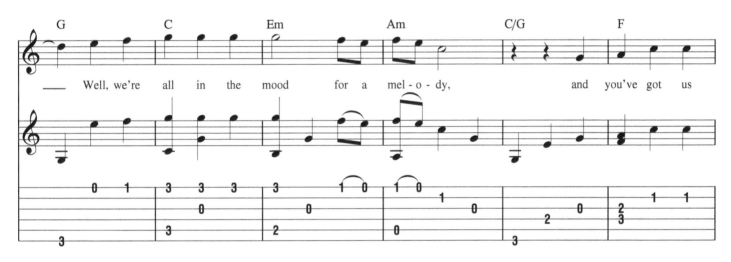

_____ Well, we're all in the mood for a mel - o - dy, and you've got us

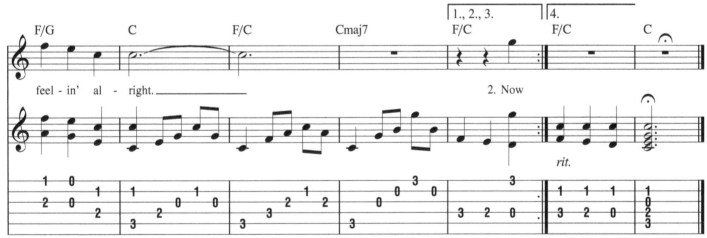

feel - in' al - right. _____ 2. Now

rit.

Additional Lyrics

2. Now John at the bar is a friend of mine, he gets me my drinks for free.
   And he's quick with a joke or to light up your smoke, but there's someplace that he'd rather be.
   He says, "Bill, I believe this is killing me," as a smile ran away from his face.
   "Well, I'm sure that I could be a movie star if I could get out of this place."

3. Now Paul is a real estate novelist, who never had time for a wife.
   And he's talking with Davy, who's still in the Navy and probably will be for life.
   And the waitress is practicing politics, as the bus'nessmen slowly get stoned.
   Yes, they're sharing a drink they call loneliness, but it's better than drinkin' alone.

4. It's pretty good crowd for a Saturday, and the manager gives me a smile.
   'Cause he knows that it's me they've been comin' to see to forget about life for a while.
   And the piano sounds like a carnival and the microphone smells like a beer.
   And they sit at the bar and put bread in my jar and say, "Man what are you doin' here?"

Sorry Seems to Be the Hardest Word

Words and Music by Elton John and Bernie Taupin

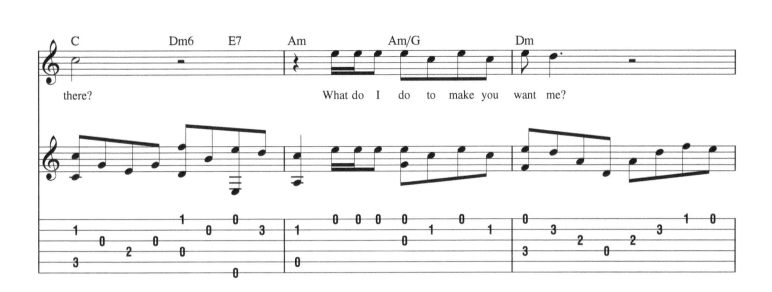

there? What do I do to make you want me?

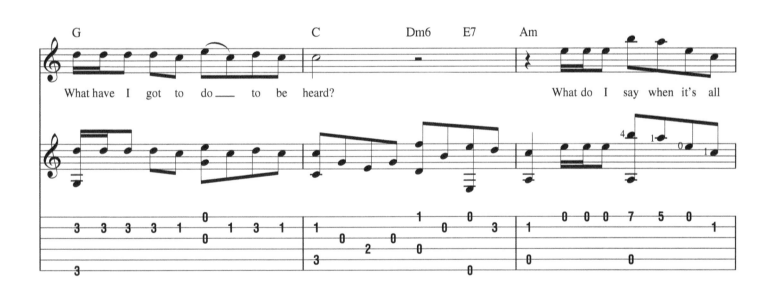

What have I got to do ___ to be heard? What do I say when it's all

o - ver? Sor - ry seems to be the hard - est word.

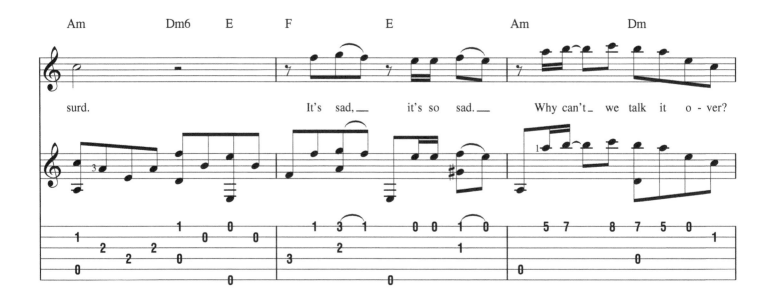

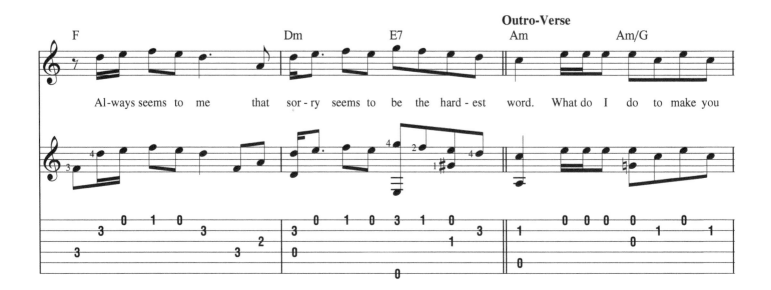

love me? What have I got to do ___ to be heard?

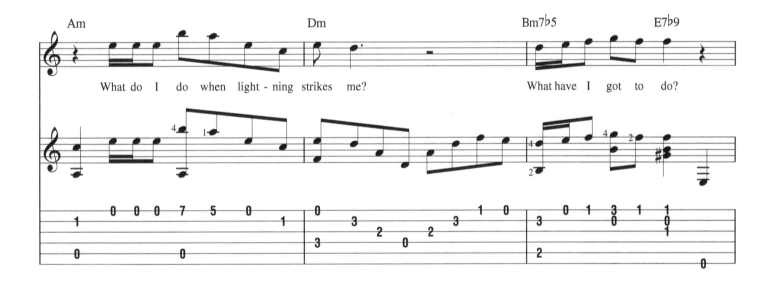

What do I do when light-ning strikes me? What have I got to do?

What have I got to do? ___ Sor-ry seems to be the hard-est word. ___

We've Only Just Begun

Words and Music by Roger Nichols and Paul Williams

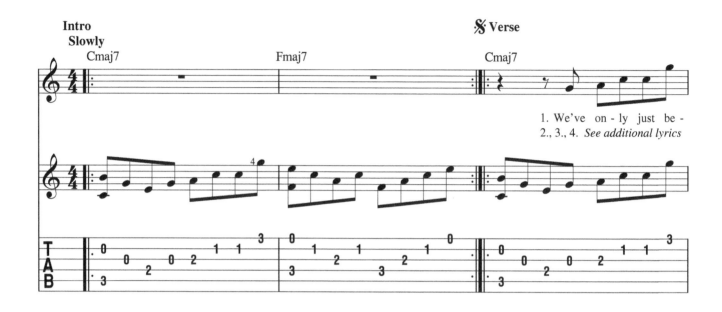

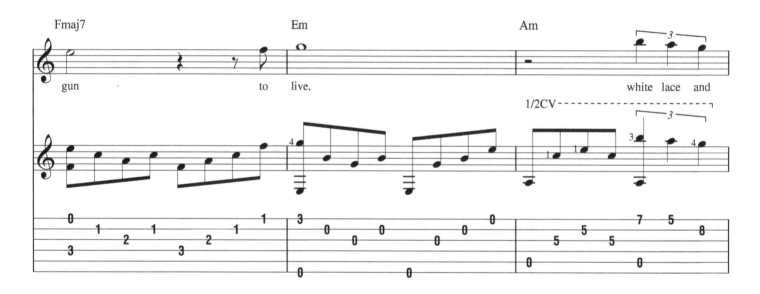

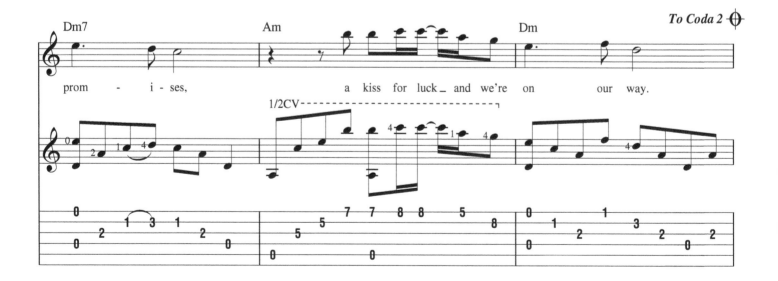

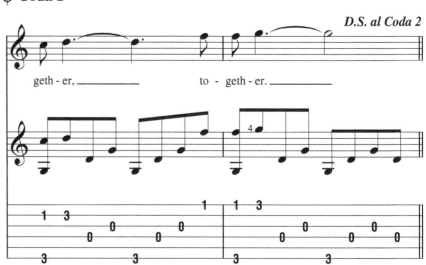

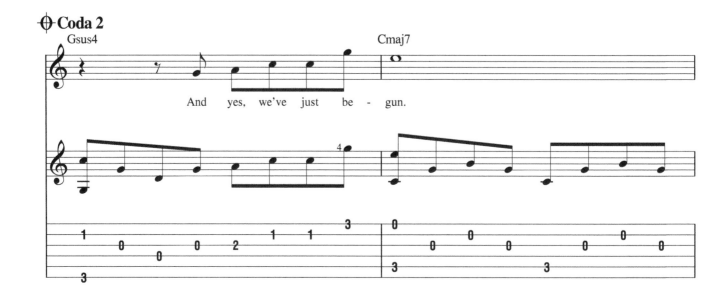

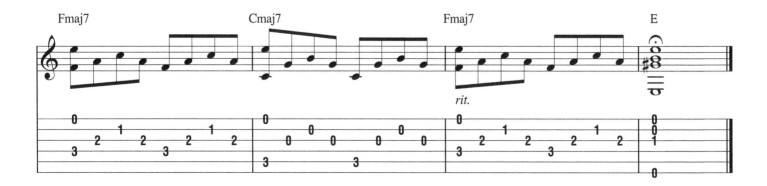

Additional Lyrics

2. Before the rising sun we fly,
   So many roads to choose,
   We start out walking and learn to run.
   And yes, we've just begun.

3., 4. And when the evening comes we smile,
   So much of life ahead,
   We'll find a place where there's room to grow.
   And yes, we've just begun.

Wonderful Tonight

Words and Music by Eric Clapton

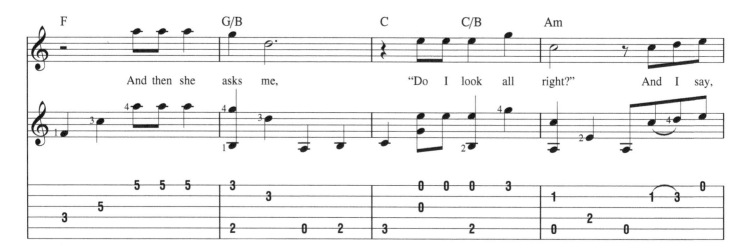

And then she asks me, "Do I look all right?" And I say,

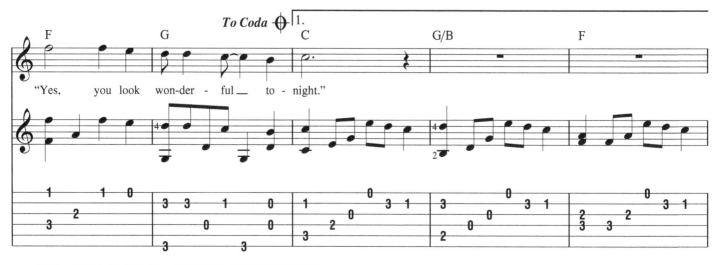

To Coda ⊕ | 1.

"Yes, you look won-der-ful ___ to-night."

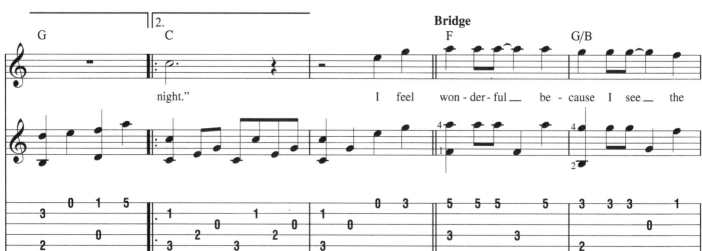

| 2.

Bridge

night." I feel won-der-ful ___ be-cause I see ___ the

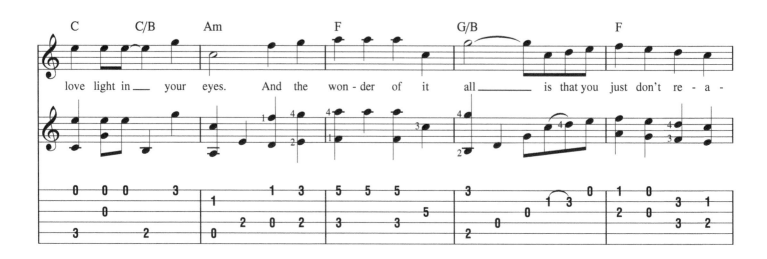

love light in ___ your eyes. And the won-der of it all ___ is that you just don't re-a-

lize how much _ I love you.

night.   Oh, my dar-ling, you were won-der-ful _ to -

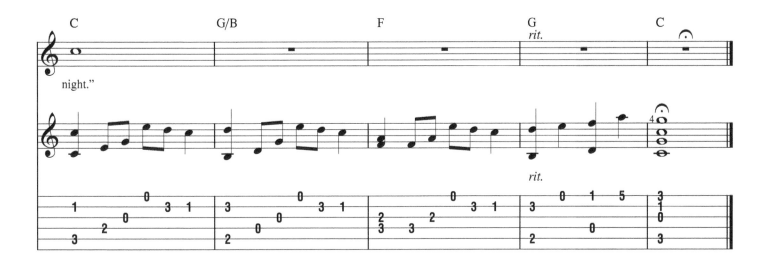

night."

Additional Lyrics

2. We go to a party, and everyone turns to see
This beautiful lady that's walking around with me.
And then she asks me, "Do you feel all right?"
And I say, "Yes, I feel wonderful tonight."

3. It's time to go home now, and I've got an aching head,
So I give her the car keys; she helps me to bed.
And then I tell her, as I turn out the light,
I say, "My darlin', you were wonderful tonight.
Oh, my darlin', you were wonderful tonight."

FINGERPICKING GUITAR BOOKS

Hone your fingerpicking skills with these great songbooks featuring solo guitar arrangements in standard notation and tablature. The arrangements in these books are carefully written for intermediate-level guitarists. Each song combines melody and harmony in one superb guitar fingerpicking arrangement. Each book also includes an introduction to basic fingerstyle guitar.

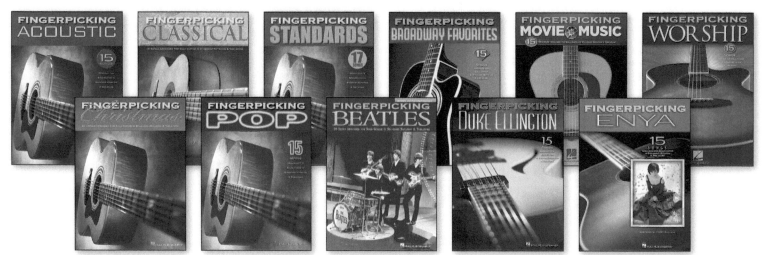

FINGERPICKING ACOUSTIC
00699614......................................$14.99

FINGERPICKING ACOUSTIC CLASSICS
00160211......................................$14.99

FINGERPICKING ACOUSTIC HITS
00160202......................................$12.99

FINGERPICKING ACOUSTIC ROCK
00699764......................................$12.99

FINGERPICKING BALLADS
00699717......................................$12.99

FINGERPICKING BEATLES
00699049......................................$19.99

FINGERPICKING BEETHOVEN
00702390..$8.99

FINGERPICKING BLUES
00701277 ....$9.99

FINGERPICKING BROADWAY FAVORITES
00699843..$9.99

FINGERPICKING BROADWAY HITS
00699838..$7.99

FINGERPICKING CELTIC FOLK
00701148......................................$10.99

FINGERPICKING CHILDREN'S SONGS
00699712..$9.99

FINGERPICKING CHRISTIAN
00701076 ....$7.99

FINGERPICKING CHRISTMAS
00699599..$9.99

FINGERPICKING CHRISTMAS CLASSICS
00701695..$7.99

FINGERPICKING CHRISTMAS SONGS
00171333..$9.99

FINGERPICKING CLASSICAL
00699620......................................$10.99

FINGERPICKING COUNTRY
00699687......................................$10.99

FINGERPICKING DISNEY
00699711......................................$15.99

FINGERPICKING EARLY JAZZ STANDARDS
00276565 ....$12.99

FINGERPICKING DUKE ELLINGTON
00699845..$9.99

FINGERPICKING ENYA
00701161......................................$10.99

FINGERPICKING FILM SCORE MUSIC
00160143......................................$12.99

FINGERPICKING GOSPEL
00701059..$9.99

FINGERPICKING GUITAR BIBLE
00691040 ....$19.99

FINGERPICKING HIT SONGS
00160195......................................$12.99

FINGERPICKING HYMNS
00699688..$9.99

FINGERPICKING IRISH SONGS
00701965..$9.99

FINGERPICKING ITALIAN SONGS
00159778......................................$12.99

FINGERPICKING JAZZ FAVORITES
00699844..$9.99

FINGERPICKING JAZZ STANDARDS
00699840......................................$10.99

FINGERPICKING ELTON JOHN
00237495......................................$12.99

FINGERPICKING LATIN FAVORITES
00699842..$9.99

FINGERPICKING LATIN STANDARDS
00699837......................................$12.99

FINGERPICKING ANDREW LLOYD WEBBER
00699839......................................$14.99

FINGERPICKING LOVE SONGS
00699841......................................$12.99

FINGERPICKING LOVE STANDARDS
00699836 ....$9.99

FINGERPICKING LULLABYES
00701276..$9.99

FINGERPICKING MOVIE MUSIC
00699919......................................$10.99

FINGERPICKING MOZART
00699794..$9.99

FINGERPICKING POP
00699615......................................$12.99

FINGERPICKING POPULAR HITS
00139079......................................$12.99

FINGERPICKING PRAISE
00699714......................................$10.99

FINGERPICKING ROCK
00699716......................................$12.99

FINGERPICKING STANDARDS
00699613......................................$12.99

FINGERPICKING WEDDING
00699637..$9.99

FINGERPICKING WORSHIP
00700554......................................$10.99

FINGERPICKING NEIL YOUNG – GREATEST HITS
00700134......................................$14.99

FINGERPICKING YULETIDE
00699654..$9.99

HAL•LEONARD®

Visit Hal Leonard online at **www.halleonard.com**